ACTIVISM IN ACTION
······ A HISTORY™ ·······

THE FIGHT FOR
DISABILITY RIGHTS

LISA A. CRAYTON

Rosen
YA™
New York

Published in 2020 by The Rosen Publishing Group, Inc.
29 East 21st Street, New York, NY 10010

First Edition

Library of Congress Cataloging-in-Publication Data

Names: Crayton, Lisa A., author.
Title: The fight for disability rights / Lisa A. Crayton.
Description: First edition. | New York : Rosen Publishing, 2020.
| Series: Activism in action : a history | Includes bibliographi-
cal references and index.
Identifiers: LCCN 2018015262| ISBN 9781508185444 (library
bound) | ISBN 9781508185437 (pbk.)
Subjects: LCSH: People with disabilities—Juvenile literature. |
People with disabilities—Civil rights—Juvenile literature.
Classification: LCC HV1568 .C73 2019 | DDC 323.3/7—dc23
LC record available at https://lccn.loc.gov/2018015262

Manufactured in China

On the cover: Leaders do what it takes to gain ground in the
fight for disability rights, including climbing the steps of government buildings (*top*) and making their voices heard in the
Disability Pride NYC Parade (*bottom*).

CONTENTS

INTRODUCTION

Shane Burcaw knows what it's like to have a disability. He also knows the importance of embracing social activism to help in the fight for disability rights. Since age two—and for more than twenty years—Burcaw has used a wheelchair. It helps him with the complications from spinal muscular atrophy, a fatal disease that affects the muscles. Some people might be sad and hopeless if they shared the same diagnosis, but not Burcaw. He advocates for disability rights. He even founded a nonprofit organization to help bring awareness to the disease. He speaks and writes about living with a disability and shares the power of humor and positivity to help people embrace life to its fullest. His timely messages of hope despite adversity mirror those of past and current disability activists.

At one time, having a disability meant being excluded from society. People with disabilities were treated like outcasts and had few rights. The disability rights movement turned things around and challenged stereotypes. Activists refused to accept societal limitations and fought for the rights of those with disabilities. Some had their own disabilities, and some did not. But together, they changed the world.

🔒 laughingatmynightmare.com

HOME   FUNNY STUFF   5K RUN   PROGRAMS   ABOUT US   DONATE   CONTACT US!   SHOP   🛒 0

Our History

How did Laughing At My Nightmare start?

In 2011, a kid named Shane Burcaw from Bethlehem, PA started a blog to tell his life story of living with a disease that made his muscles waste away as he grew older. His stories made fun of the problems he was dealing with and people took notice.

The blog blew up, **achieving HALF A MILLION followers** (a number that still grows to this day). Shane realized how badly people needed humor in their lives, so he set out with his cousin Sarah to create a company that could help people laugh more and help others living with the same disease. The rest is history.

Laughing At My Nightmare, Inc. is a 501(c)3 nonprofit with a mission to spread a message of positivity while providing equipment grants to those living with muscular dystrophy.

Disability advocate Shane Burcaw uses humor and positivity while sharing his experience with a fatal disease, and while fighting for disability rights.

Today, it is commonly accepted that having a disability does not—and should not—stop a person from reaching his or her fullest potential. People with disabilities pursue their dreams, moving freely in society, thanks to the help of accessible transportation, braille lettering in elevators, advances in medical devices for sight, hearing, and mobility, service animals in schools and workplaces, and talk-to-text features on electronics. Moreover, people with disabilities work where they want, enjoying careers in STEM (science, technology, engineering, and mathematics). They also work in education, law enforcement, construction, fire safety, and entertainment. Really, there is no career that is off-limits to a person with a disability!

Despite the accomplishments of the disability rights movement, more can be done. There is a growing need to help maintain the rights already won and to continually advocate for those who encounter prejudice, discrimination, or injustice. Teens are needed to join the fight. In his book, *Not So Different: What You REALLY Want to Ask About Having a Disability*, Shane Burcaw writes about social stigmas. He explains: "So many of the social stigmas that people with disabilities face could be squashed if we are able to instill in young people the idea that we are all different, we all have different weaknesses, and abilities, and that's not just okay, it's beautiful." Burcaw's idea is similar to the focus of the disability rights movement. It is one teens can help to support. When they actively participate in social activism, they empower people of all ages and abilities. They affect change, altering people's perception of what being different means, and how it adds to the beauty of the world's populations. All teens can join the fight for disability rights, and by teaming up with their peers, they can make the world a better place for all of us.

CHAPTER ONE

A DIFFERENT WORLD

"Diversity" is a buzzword that is commonly used when describing a variety of people. It usually applies to race, however, it also covers gender, age, sexual orientation, and abilities. Activism has helped to change how people view all of these differences.

Socially conscious teens have played a role. They have been—and are—key to social change. They help shape public opinion about how and why it is important to accept all people—no matter what! Teens' voices and efforts are needed to continually make the world a better place for everybody, including people with disabilities.

THAT'S DIFFERENT!

Almost everything produced has something special about it that draws attention. An upgraded version of a cell phone or video system may offer opportunities to completely customize games for greater flexibility and enjoyment. A newly designed brand of athletic shoes may feature vivid colors and accents that make them more desirable than competing brands. Anticipated differences like these are usually applauded, encouraged, and welcomed. That is not the same reaction as when people unexpectedly encounter others who look, sound, act, or process things differently due to a disability. Reactions vary when people see someone with a disability. One common reaction is surprise, as people wonder about the condition. Some are courageous enough to ask about it.

REAL-LIFE WONDER

Writers often pen material based on a real-life experience. R. J. Palacio wrote her bestselling novel, *Wonder*, based on her young son's fear when he saw a girl with unique facial features. Palacio and the boy rushed away, but she later thought maybe she had missed a teachable moment that would help her son overcome the fear of differences. In an interview for *People Magazine*, Palacio recalled the experience: "That just got me thinking about what it must be like to face a world every day that doesn't quite know how to face you back."

Palacio's considerations led to the writing of *Wonder*. In it, the main character has Treacher Collins syndrome, a genetic condition affecting the face. When he starts fifth grade at the first traditional school he's ever attended, he is met with fear, bullying, and other negative responses. How he and others react is the focus of the novel, as it encourages kindness and acceptance of people with differences. The movie version of *Wonder* debuted in November 2017, receiving rave reviews. It was later nominated for an Academy Award for Best Makeup and Hairstyling.

Treating people with disabilities with kindness and acceptance is a key theme in *Wonder*, a movie based on R. J. Palacio's novel of the same name.

Others are not as brave. In some cases, onlookers are scared of disabilities. Their fears can often be tied to superstitious beliefs, but more commonly, ignorance or concerns that they might "catch" the condition. However, disabilities are not contagious, and people can't catch them like they would a cold or flu.

DISABILITIES DEFINED

A disability is a condition that affects a person's body, mind, or emotions. It causes the affected area to work differently, usually resulting in a limitation. For example, a person with vision loss may be able to see some things, or see nothing at all. There is a difference between a disability and a deformity. When a person is born with a physical condition, such as missing fingers, they are said to have a congenital deformity. The condition may not be classified as a disability if it does not restrict a person's abilities. The federal government, for example, classifies disabilities in very specific ways. Cities and states use its guidelines to uphold disability rights, while helping to provide needed resources.

Generally, many types of disabilities exist. Most people have seen someone with some sort of disability. Others have a disability, or know someone

Disabilities fall into broad categories; they include physical or internal conditions and related limitations occurring at birth or from an injury later in life.

who does, such as a relative, friend, educator, or neighbor. Conditions fall into two broad groups: physical or internal. A physical condition is anything that affects the body's senses or abilities. Hearing and vision loss are well-known conditions that affect the senses. Asthma is a common respiratory condition. Less well-known are disabilities that affect the spine or muscles, and limit mobility, such as cerebral palsy or poliomyelitis (also known as polio). An internal disability affects the mind/

brain and emotions. It's not always possible to know if someone has a condition by just looking at them. This category of disabilities includes autism and Down syndrome. Dyslexia, attention-deficit/hyperactivity disorder (ADHD), obsessive compulsive disorder (OCD), and bipolar disorder are also in this category. Autism and Down syndrome occur from mental or physical disabilities and are also considered to be developmental disabilities.

The May Institute is a nonprofit organization focusing on providing resources to people with different types of abilities. Its website states that 5.4 million US citizens have developmental disabilities. Its fact sheet on developmental disabilities explains these are life-long conditions that are usually diagnosed before a person is twenty-two years old. And, according to the May Institute, about 17 percent of youth under age 18 have a development disability.

WORDS MATTER

A disability is not a reason for people to mock or shame others, yet it happens all the time. Often people use words that hurt and harm by referring to a disability, or a person with a disability, in a mean way. For example, people with mental

disabilities may be called "crazy" or "psycho." Sometimes, derogatory terms for disabilities are used in light-hearted ways. This can include telling a joke, or saying "that's crazy" to a story that seems unbelievable. The truth is that words matter. Using such terms in casual ways is not okay, as they diminish the real struggles—and victories—people with disabilities have had in living with their conditions. These terms also reinforce stereotypes, hurt feelings, and make it more difficult for those with disabilities to gain the respect they deserve. Refrain from language that is insensitive to people with disabilities, and help others to understand the importance of doing the same. Teens can empower themselves and others to be advocates for people with disabilities.

New inventions help people with disabilities; here a Lynden, Washington, high school student with a disabling condition of the spine tests an invention developed by her peers.

WHO IS AFFECTED

Disabilities affect kids, teens, and adults of all races and backgrounds. All nations have citizens who have disabilities. According to Disabled-World.com, an independent source of news about disabilities, about 10 percent of people worldwide have a disability. In the United States, the Centers for Disease Control and Prevention (CDC) is the federal government agency responsible for protecting against and responding to health-related threats. It reports that 22 percent of adult citizens have some form of disability. The interesting thing about physical and internal types of disabilities is that they affect people differently. Food allergies, for example, can cause minor irritations or they can kill a person who comes in contact with the allergen.

CAUSES OF DISABILITIES

What causes disabilities? A physical condition may occur from various sources, including:

- **Birth complications**. Sometimes, something goes wrong when a baby is being born. He or she may suffer an injury that

When students with and without disabilities team up, such as on a cheerleading squad, they help debunk stereotypes about disabilities and promote acceptance.

results in a disability. Seizure disorders, spinal conditions, and brain injuries fall into this category.

- **Family Health.** If a relative has a condition, or carries a gene for it, a child may be born with that same condition. Sickle-cell anemia, Down syndrome, and heart conditions are just some examples.
- **Illness**. An illness may lead to a disability. Juvenile diabetes, cancer, high fevers in a

child, and lead poisoning are some causes of illness-related disabilities.

- **Injury**. Injuries can occur at birth. Other injuries happen later in life. For example, sports injuries can cause brain damage, paralysis, and other conditions. Injuries from car accidents also cause disabilities, rendering people unable to move, speak, or mentally process. Falling from an open window, off a skateboard, or down a flight of stairs may result in a child, teen, or adult having a disability.
- **Other**. Smoking, illegal drug use, obesity, and other factors can cause disabling conditions. For example, a nineteen-year-old rugby player in Australia ate a garden slug as a dare in 2010 and was permanently paralyzed from a brain infection! The slug looked ordinary, but it carried a parasite common to rats. The parasite caused the brain infection. In March 2018, his mother was fighting for the right for him to continue to receive much-needed health benefits for his condition.

These sources of disabilities prove that anyone is at risk of having a disability. Because of the many contributing factors, it's important to understand disabilities and join the fight for disability rights. For example, health care is just one area in which disability rights advocates—whether family members or strangers—are needed to help defend and secure rights for people with disabilities.

People of all abilities and ages have been involved in the fight for disability rights since the movement began decades ago. Teens have played important roles in this movement. Their daring support of people with disabilities has contributed to positive change over the years. Teen activism helps to spark awareness of specific conditions, debunk myths, fight stereotypes, and make the world a better place for everyone.

CHAPTER TWO

HIDDEN FIGURES

W hen Lizzie Velasquez was in high school, she experienced a life-altering case of cyberbullying from YouTube viewers calling her "The World's Ugliest Woman." Some suggested she should kill herself. Others called her demeaning names. What made strangers bully her in such a cruel way? They were negatively reacting to the seventeen-year-old's unique appearance, which had been affected by a disability. Velasquez was born with a rare condition—neonatal progeroid syndrome— affecting only two other known living people in the world as of March 2018. It affects her heart, bones, eyes, and ability to gain weight. As a result, she has complete vision loss in one eye and some vision loss in the other. Plus, Velasquez is very slender, weighing less than 70 pounds (32 kilograms).

The horrible cyberbullying video about Velasquez went viral, attracting millions of views. However, if the traumatic attack was supposed to make her hide from the world, it backfired. In a TEDxAustinWomen talk called "How Do YOU

Lizzie Velasquez survived a horrendous case of cyberbullying targeted at her disability and became a staunch antibullying and disability rights advocate.

Define Yourself," she explained how the experience shaped the way she defines herself by goals, not a disability. Velasquez said, "I started realizing, am I going to let the people who called me a monster, define me? ... No, I'm going to let my goals and my success and my accomplishments be the things that define me." The December 2013 video of the presentation has been viewed more than thirteen million times.

FIGHTING STEREOTYPES

Lizzie Velasquez initially set goals to become a college graduate, motivational speaker, and author. In more than a decade since the ugly cyberbullying attack, she has beautifully achieved—and exceeded—her initial goals. She became an internet sensation, the creator of a popular YouTube channel visited by millions of people worldwide, and a talk show host for Unzipped beginning in 2017.

Lizzie's bullying experience reveals three things about the stereotypes surrounding disabilities. First, when a disability is recognized, it can attract negative attention. Second, having a disability need not limit a person's ability to set and achieve goals. And third, although someone with a disability may look, sound, or act differently, he or she is deserving of respect, access to needed resources, and opportunities to pursue dream jobs and careers.

EFFECTS OF WRONG PERCEPTIONS

When people think about disabilities, many things come to mind, many of which are incorrect. They are based on historical stereotypes, labeling people with disabilities as broken, useless, or incapable of feelings or thought. Attitudes based on stereotypes about disabilities have led to: 1) widespread negative attitudes; 2) historical treatment as second-class citizens; and 3) a long-lasting disability stigma.

NEGATIVE ATTITUDES

Disabilities have existed for centuries, much like the negative attitudes that have been shared in reaction to them. People with disabilities were considered freaks of nature, and treated as if they also had a disabling condition that affected the mind or emotions. A disability was seen as affecting the entire person, and people with disabilities were sometimes thought to have curses that could harm others. For example, some thought disabilities were caused by the moon. "Lunacy," a form of the word "lunar" which refers to the moon, was a term used for mental disability. People having a mental disability were called "lunatics." Today, this term is considered to be derogatory, and is avoided when describing one with a mental disability.

SECOND-CLASS CITIZENS

People with disabilities were often shunned, hidden, denied access, treated unfairly,

Historically, many people with mental disabilities were confined in psychiatric hospitals. They were forced to wear straitjackets, garments that limited their mobility.

and excluded from society. Many were placed in special institutions for people with physical or mental conditions. Those places were not helpful and did not provide the services needed to help patients thrive while overcoming their limitations. In many cases, conditions were horrible in the institutions, and were unsafe to live in. Patients were given just the basic necessities to keep them alive. They became social outcasts, excluded from society and not afforded the same privileges as other citizens. They became known as "second-class citizens."

LONG-LASTING STIGMA

A stigma is a negative belief—usually based on faulty and inaccurate information—about a person or concept. Entire groups of people, such as minorities or those with disabilities, suffer from negative actions based on stigmas. One such stigma is being defined by one's condition. Rather than being seen as smart, important, and useful, people with disabilities are often viewed only by their limitations. While a disability can cause a limitation, it is just a condition. It does not define a person's intelligence, skills, compassion, hopes, dreams, or importance.

FACING BARRIERS

Historically, barriers resulted from the way people with disabilities were treated. They were denied access to basic things other citizens enjoyed, such as much-needed health care, education, and the freedom to go where they wanted to go within a community. Families were also greatly impacted. Indeed, many people with disabilities were excluded from basic interactions with family and neighbors, because their relatives were ashamed of them. Thus, little was done to help them navigate and enjoy the world around them. Even if they did go out into the community, they had problems getting here and there. Poorly designed roads, buildings, and transportation made it hard to get around. Changes to architecture, structures, and transportation were greatly needed to make the nation more accessible.

People with disabilities also faced discrimination in employment. Most were prevented from working, and there were severe limitations to what they were allowed to do. Some jobs placed people with disabilities in situations where they were subjected to ridicule. For example, they became spectacles when working for circuses and were mocked by circus goers. Work environments like these did not foster acceptance or understanding, but rather reinforced negative stereotypes.

Helen Keller lost her sight after a childhood accident. She became famous for overcoming related limitations and for helping people better understand vision loss.

HOPE EMERGES

In the midst of oppressive environments, hope began to emerge. One of the pivotal changes was sparked by resources established to help people with disabilities. Gallaudet University opened in Washington, DC, in 1864 to help educate people with hearing loss, particularly those who were deaf. The university remains open today and serves as a beacon of inspiration for potential and current students. In 1921, the American Foundation for the Blind was established. Helen Keller was a spokesperson—also known as an ambassador—for the organization that continues its advocacy today.

Other positive signs of change were inspired by various advocates and organizations, one of whom was Franklin D. Roosevelt. He was paralyzed after getting polio at the age of thirty-nine. He required a wheelchair for the remainder

CONNECTED BY FILM

Helen Keller was a young girl when an accident caused her to lose vision in both eyes. She lived during a time when people with disabilities were considered useless. Her parents felt differently. They hired a live-in teacher who helped Keller learn to read braille and write. Over time, Keller's accomplishments attracted worldwide attention. She traveled and spoke about how blindness affects people, helping address stereotypes about people with disabilities. She also wrote a book about her life.

Patty Duke is an actress who has played roles as Helen Keller in a play and a film. At the age of seventeen, Patty played Keller in the 1965 television movie, *The Miracle Worker*. It focused on how Keller's teacher helped her and challenged people's beliefs about those with disabilities. Duke made history as one of the youngest people to receive an Academy Award when she won for Best Supporting Actress for her performance. In 1982, Duke was diagnosed with manic depression (now referred to as bipolar disorder), a serious brain disorder. Over the years, she has assumed another role, that of a disability advocate who publicly shares her condition and other mental disabilities.

of his life, but it didn't stop him from becoming the thirty-second president of the United States in 1933. He remained in office until his death in 1945. Roosevelt was a disability rights advocate. In 1938, he helped launch the National Foundation for Infantile Paralysis, now called the March of Dimes. Its initial focus was on advocating for a cure for polio. After a successful vaccine was developed by Dr. Jonas Salk in 1953, the March of Dimes expanded its focus to addressing other disorders affecting babies. Today, the organization

US president Franklin D. Roosevelt was paralyzed after contracting polio as an adult. He and his wife, Eleanor, are pictured here with children who also have polio-related disabilities.

continues its advocacy on behalf of babies and pregnant women.

In 1940, the National Federation of the Blind was started in Wilkes-Barre, Pennsylvania, by a group of individuals who were blind. Jacobus tenBroek, a lawyer in California, was the first president of the foundation. Unlike many others with visual disabilities at that time, he achieved a high level of career success. The National Federation of the Blind succeeded in advocating for resources, and in changing perceptions about people with vision loss. Its early successes proved useful to other organizations, as they began addressing other types of disabilities. The organization remains actively involved in the fight for disability rights.

CHAPTER THREE

THE ROAD TO INCLUSION

· · · · · · · · · · · · · · ● ● ● ● ● ● · · · · · · · · · ·

R iding a bicycle is a fun, physical activity for kids and adults. Few, however, rode 400 miles (644 kilometers) across their country to raise awareness about disabilities and the power of overcoming limitations. But that's exactly what athlete, Emmanuel Ofosu Yeboah, did! He was born in Ghana in 1977 without a tibia in his right leg. (A tibia is the second-largest bone in the leg.) In his country, being born "different" had long been considered a curse. Many people with disabilities were shunned and forced into lives of extreme poverty. With only one functioning leg, the young man was destined by society to a future of begging for the rest of his life. However, his mother raised him to dream big and believe he could have a fulfilling life. Learning to ride a bike empowered his mobility. After the death of his mother, Yeboah requested and received a bike from a California nonprofit organization. It helped to power his dream of riding across his country to bring awareness. Yeboah dedicated his 2002 ten-day bike ride

Emmanuel Ofosu Yeboah's successful 400-mile (644 km) trek across Ghana on a bicycle helped change Ghana's views about disabilities and sparked a change in its laws.

to his mother. He was cheered along on his journey, and once his ride was completed, Yeboah was considered an international hero.

Yeboah has since competed in international athletic competitions, and won awards from Nike, ESPN, and other organizations. He also had surgery in the US in 2003, in an effort to amputate part of his leg. He was fitted for a prosthetic leg. Famous celebrity Oprah Winfrey narrated a 2005 documentary about his life. Yeboah also appeared on her former TV show. Books have also been written about his inspiring life.

Thanks in part to Yeboah's bike ride and activism, Ghana enacted the Persons with Disabilities Act in 2006. It granted more rights to people with disabilities. Today, Yeboah continues to be actively involved in the fight for disability rights through a foundation he started. It provides a variety of resources to people with disabilities. Its mission, according to his website, is "[t]o change society by empowering people with disabilities."

Emmanuel Yeboah's story reveals some key facts about disabilities. First, they occur all over the world. Second, they happen at various times in one's life. Third, and most importantly, disabilities may be limiting but do not have to be totally restrictive. In his words, "Disability is not inability." Having a bicycle initially helped Yeboah's mobility, but surgery and a prosthetic leg granted him freedom.

DIFFERENT AND HIDDEN

Much like the young Emmanuel Ofosu Yeboah growing up in Ghana, Americans with disabilities were kept from living full, happy lives. A wall of exclusion separated them from family. They weren't free to dream about what they wanted to do in life, because society did not make room for them to be active, involved citizens. The only way to make them visible, active citizens was assuring they had access in every area of life. That could not happen until people realized there was a problem, and until concerned individuals joined forces to make real, lasting change. Disability rights advocates stepped

JUST A LIMITATION

A disability, regardless of the type, is a limitation that can restrict a person's mobility, making it difficult to stand or walk. It can affect a person's mind, making it difficult to think or process information.

Affected individuals may have limited or no ability to perform other day-to-day activities. A disability may make it hard for teens and adults to cook, drive, or use household gadgets. Other potential limitations include:

- Moving or controlling one or more body parts
- Thinking clearly
- Processing information
- Getting out of bed
- Washing or dressing
- Eating
- Standing
- Walking
- Learning
- Reading
- Writing
- Focusing on classwork

up to help and spur change. Their efforts pushed disability-related topics to the top of important concerns to Americans. Soon, people questioned why being different also meant being hidden. They were challenged to rethink how they viewed people with disabilities. Access became the focus. However, obtaining this access was not an easy fight. There were too many barriers in place, and governments, companies, and other entities felt they could not afford to spend money to provide structural or other changes. The answer? Get laws passed that assured long-term access and toppled restrictions.

INSPIRATION FROM THE CIVIL RIGHTS MOVEMENT

Disability rights activists drew inspiration from the civil rights movement in the United States. From the 1950s to the mid-1960s, the activists in the movement pushed for equality and inclusion for African Americans. They used various means to win victories. People of different genders, races, and backgrounds teamed up to help. Nonviolence was a key strategy. Protests included sit-ins, boycotts, marches, and voting registration drives. They peacefully demanded national change. The Freedom Rides, for example, sought changes in interstate travel throughout the country. They put the spotlight on America's racial divide, especially with problems in the South.

Famous civil rights activists joined lesser known activists in helping to spur the passage of key civil rights laws. The Civil Rights Act of 1964 and the Voting Rights Act of 1965 were huge accomplishments made possible by the efforts of civil rights activists. The world was watching as these gains were achieved. Disability rights advocates also took notice. They realized that some of the same

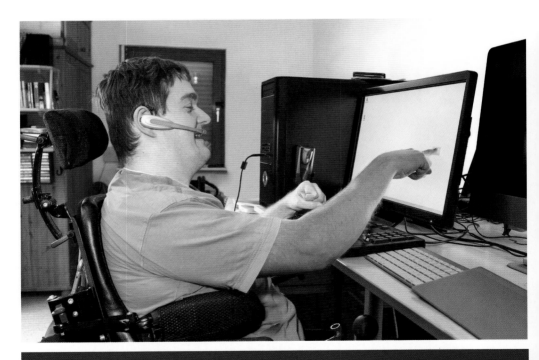

A disability is only a limitation. Thanks to the fight for disability rights, people with disabilities have available tools and technologies to help them succeed in every area of life.

issues addressed by the civil rights movement also affected people with disabilities. Those included:

- **Employment**. People with disabilities needed to work. They also needed skills to get and keep jobs. They needed workplaces free from discrimination and accessible for people with disabilities.
- **Housing**. People with disabilities wanted to live on their own, but needed housing with accessible features so they could function despite limitations. More so, housing had to be free from harassment or discrimination.
- **Education**. Schools and classrooms were targeted for change. The need for safe schools where students could learn in accommodating environments became a top priority.

Civil rights legislation did not necessarily address issues specific to disabilities. Yet, as the laws were written, they could be—and were—used to help argue for access and resources. The Freedom Riders of the early 1960s, for example, rode buses to challenge segregation laws that made it dangerous and humiliating for African Americans to travel, especially in the South. When those laws were toppled, black passengers could ride freely without harassment. Safe, accessible transportation was a must, and buses, taxis, trains, and other motor vehicles had to be easier to use. People with disabilities used special equipment, including wheelchairs, walkers, or service animals that could not be left at home. Gaining access to transportation meant being able to have these helpful resources with them.

MUSEUM OF DISABILITY HISTORY

Where can students learn more about disabilities? One place is at museums that provide means for people to experience the past or present through unique exhibits and artistic performances. One such location is the Museum of disABILITY History in Buffalo, New York. It opened in 1988, and according to its website, advances "the understanding, acceptance and independence of people with disabilities." It offers exhibits, collections, and special programs. Online, the museum provides other fascinating resources. Virtual exhibits provide understanding of different events in history, including effective organizations and activists. Other website material features "Inside

Scoop" pages on specific disabilities, tips, and a quiz about myths and misconceptions. Virtual visitors can also shop its store for a wide variety of DVDs, books, and gift items.

The Museum of disABILITY History provides many resources and exhibits that provide a historic view of the fight for disability rights.

ACHIEVING INDEPENDENT LIVING

Historically, people with disabilities did not live on their own. There were few housing options that allowed them to live easily and safely. Disability

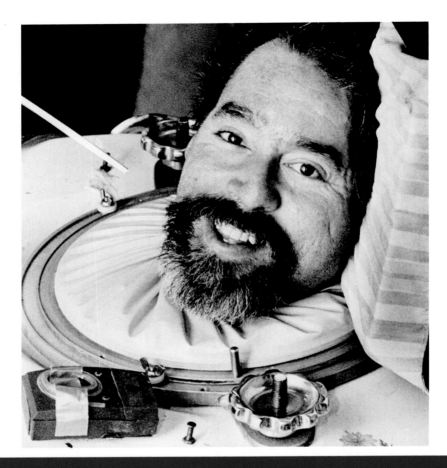

An iron lung is a medical device that aids in breathing. Ed Roberts, who brought awareness of access issues faced by people with disabilities, used one daily because of lingering complications from polio.

rights advocates fought for the rights of adults with disabilities to live on their own and receive assistance if needed. The first Center for Independent Living opened in 1972, led by Ed Roberts. He was a former student at the University of California,

Berkeley, and a polio survivor. Roberts contracted the paralyzing virus when he was a teenager, and because he was a quadriplegic, needed the use of a wheelchair.

At first, the teenager was prevented from attending his local high school, but his family successfully pushed for his admittance. Then he encountered a similar resistance while applying for college. In 1962, however, the University of California, Berkeley, accepted Roberts for admission. It was a major win for him and for all students with disabilities. But he still faced accessibility challenges. Roberts had trouble getting around the campus, as it was not designed for wheelchairs. Plus, there were no elevators. He didn't give up. The young man stayed in school, and received excellent grades. His academic success inspired the university to accept other students with disabilities. Unfortunately, the students faced the same barriers Roberts had faced: a lack of accessible structures and staff members familiar enough with disabilities to help.

In 1970, Roberts received a grant. He used the monies to start a program at the school to help students with disabilities. Staff made up of those with disabilities was hired and they offered vital assistance and counseling. When nonstudents learned about the program, they wanted to lend a helping hand. Roberts responded by opening the Center for Independent Living in 1972. It was a huge success, and is credited for advancing the world's attention on independent living.

CAREER MOVES

Around the same time as Roberts was advocating in California, polio survivor Judy Heumann was across the country in New York, waging and winning her own accessibility fights. She wanted to teach in New York but was told she could not because of her disability. She sued for discrimination and won. Her victory caused others to connect with Heumman for help with their own career-related concerns. Wanting to help, Heumman started Disabled in Action (DIA) in 1970. It focused on political action and protests. DIA's efforts were successful, drawing media attention to the plight of people with disabilities. DIA's actions made the nation more aware of some of the access issues facing people with disabilities.

CHAPTER FOUR

ACCESS GRANTED

． ． ． ． ． ． ． ． ． ● ● ● ● ● ● ● ● ● ● ． ． ． ．

For decades, musician, composer, and singer, Stevie Wonder, has won the hearts of music lovers worldwide. But he is not just an entertainer—he's an advocate for various causes, especially disability rights. Born six weeks premature, Steveland Hardaway Judkins experienced complete vision loss soon after due to an eye condition. Yet, the disability did not hinder his growing enthusiasm for music. He began playing music at age four, and it was clear that he had great talent. He could play several instruments by the time he was nine years old and was already showing signs of being a gifted singer. He landed his first recording contract at age eleven.

In Wonder's career, which has spanned more than five decades, he has won twenty-five Grammy Awards, the music industry's highest achievement. He also won an Academy Award, the film industry's highest award. Wonder was inducted into the Rock and Roll Hall of Fame in

1989. The next year, the United Nations named Stevie Wonder a "Messenger of Peace," with a focus on "championing people with disabilities." UN Secretary-General Ban Ki-moon announced his appointment, saying "Stevie Wonder is a true inspiration to young people all over the world about what can be achieved despite any physical limitations."

In 2014, US president Barack Obama awarded Wonder the Presidential Medal of Freedom, the highest award given to a civilian citizen. Today, while still sharing his musical gifts with the world,

Stevie Wonder, one of America's most prolific, award-winning musicians, accepts the Presidential Medal of Freedom from US president Barack Obama in 2014.

Stevie Wonder continues to be an advocate for disability rights. His success highlights several things. First, different causes, such as being born prematurely, can cause disabilities in infants. Second, a physical disability may affect a body part, but does not hinder a person's creativity. And third, music and other art forms can be powerful instruments in the fight for disability rights.

PROTESTING FOR CHANGE

The Rehabilitation Act of 1973 expanded rights for people with disabilities. It included a section that dramatically advanced access in the US. Section 504 was modeled after the 1964 Civil Rights Act, and sought civil rights protection for people with disabilities. It stated, "No otherwise qualified individual ... shall, solely by reason of his or her disability, be excluded from the participation in, be denied the benefits of, or be subjected to discrimination under any program or activity receiving federal financial assistance." In other words, Section 504 required that any entity receiving federal funds had to be accessible to those with disabilities.

If the Rehabilitation Act of 1973 became law, it would affect practically every type of community resource, including parks, schools, community centers, stores, restaurants, and tourist attractions. All of these would have to make structural and other improvements to ensure access to people with disabilities. Section 504 was a major victory, but there was a catch. The anticipated costs associated were used as a reason for delaying its implementation. Joseph Anthony Califano Jr., the US Secretary of Health, Education, and Welfare (HEW) at the time, was responsible for signing and implementing the Act. But he did nothing. After four years of inaction, disability rights advocates had had enough.

On April 5, 1977, demonstrations were

Chris Brewer (*left*) and Karen Emerson (*right*), who were among the disability rights activists protesting in San Francisco, celebrate the news that important regulations were signed on April 28, 1977.

held to protest the delay. At HEW headquarters in Washington, DC, Frank Bowe and hundreds of other people with disabilities spent twenty-four hours in Califano's office. Across the country, Judy Heumann and other well-known disability rights activists took over HEW's San Francisco office for twenty-five days. People involved in the demonstrations represented different genders, races, ages, and economic backgrounds. While they worked indoors, other advocates held outdoor demonstrations. In addition, food, blankets, cots, and other items were delivered to those inside by organizations like the Salvation Army, activist groups like the Black Panthers, churches, community groups, and concerned citizens. The media extensively covered the protests, and with the collective support, protesters were encouraged to hold out for change. As a result, Califano signed the Section 504 regulations on April 28, 1977.

In a 2017 article about the protests, disability rights advocate Corbett Joan O'Toole reflected on the successful protests. She noted:

> When we left the building, we each individually believed that we had made it happen…. people inside and outside the building, and in the community at large, felt like we took on the federal government and won. After that, nothing felt like an obstacle.

WHO WROTE THAT?

Writing has power—it can either reinforce or debunk stereotypes about people with disabilities. Take, for instance, scripts, articles, novels, nonfiction books, comic strips, and blogs. They can be destructive, making it harder for featured groups to deal with attitudes or actions based on false perceptions. Or, they can celebrate diversity, making it easier for groups to live free from discrimination.

Over the past few years, the publishing industry has been under fire to provide access to people who are writing from their own experiences. Why? Because much of what's been written about such groups is not penned by members of those groups. Disability rights activists are joining in the call for more material from writers with disabilities—and with various types of conditions. The publishing industry is responding through various projects to help those writers who have been marginalized have access to publishers and contracts for their writing. This is good news for all writers!

ACCESSIBLE EDUCATION FOR ALL

Before Section 504 was signed, other efforts were underway to expand access in education. In 1975, thanks to successful advocacy efforts, Public Law 94-142 Education of All Handicapped Children Act became law. It required that students with disabilities be educated in an environment with the "least restrictions." In many respects, this opened the door for many students with disabilities to learn outside of resource rooms or special education classes. Additionally, it led to schools adopting specific procedures to help them succeed in school.

READY, WILLING, AND ABLE

Gallaudet University was founded in 1864 to provide higher education for people with hearing disabilities, particularly those who were deaf. Up until 1988, however, the university had never had a president with a hearing disability. That year, when the position of president opened up, another person without a disability was hired. Students were unhappy with the university's reason for not hiring a person with a disability. Their concerns were brushed aside. In response, they teamed up with faculty and

I. King Jordan addresses a crowd of protesting Gallaudet University students. He was hired in 1988 as the school's first deaf president and retired in 2006.

began protesting. Their successful efforts led to the school's closing for a week. As a result, I. King Jordan was named the new president. Jordan, who is deaf, was no stranger to faculty and students. He had served as dean of students at Gallaudet. As president, he served for eighteen years until his retirement in 2006. The successful activism at Gallaudet University in 1988 proved that students with disabilities were ready, willing, and able to be more actively involved in their educations.

RIGHTS AND ROLES

As the protests against delaying Section 504 regulations demonstrated, the media has been active in capturing the fight for disability rights. And yet, the coverage hasn't always been favorable. When society believed that people with disabilities were feeble, the media amplified that false perception. As the fight for disability rights began dispelling myths and proving stereotypes wrong, the media began changing as well. More positive coverage of disabilities slowly appeared in newspapers, books, magazines, and television programs.

Hollywood was perhaps one of the greatest influences. Initially, people with disabilities were invisible in Hollywood. Patty Duke's role in *The Miracle Worker* helped, but it would be many years before more visible roles were played by people with disabilities. Also, Duke's role revealed how Hollywood might portray a disability, yet not cast a person with a disability to play that role. Although she did not have a low vision disability, Duke played Helen Keller, a famous person with total vision loss. Over time, Hollywood began using more actors with disabilities. Chris Burke's role in *Life Goes On* in the 1980s was a significant example. Burke has Down syndrome, and in 1989, landed a groundbreaking role as Corky, a character with Down syndrome on the television series. An article about his role appeared in the November 1, 1989, issue of *Life* magazine. The headline on the cover read, "A Special Kind of Hero: A TV Actor with Down Syndrome Steals America's Heart."

The selection of Chris Burke (*right*) as a *Life Goes On* cast member enabled him to fight stereotypes and paved the way for other actors with disabilities to land TV roles.

Burke starred in the series throughout its four seasons on air. His acting dramatically changed how people viewed people with disabilities. After the series ended, Burke landed other acting work while continuing to serve as a disability rights advocate. His role as Corky made it possible for other acting professionals with disabilities to work professionally. Lauren Potter, for example, played Becky Jackson on the television series, *Glee*. Potter also has Down syndrome and is a disability rights advocate.

Jamie Brewer has become another high-profile figure and advocate. To begin with, the actress and model has starred in plays, movies, and the multiple seasons of the wildly successful TV show *American Horror Story*. Then in 2015 she made history when she became the first woman with Down syndrome to hit the runway during New York Fashion Week. She was a part of the Role Models Not Runway Models show. When Brewer is not on stage, screen, or runway, she is an outspoken advocate for disability rights. She even held the position of president of the Arc, the nation's largest organization advocating for those (and their families) with physical and intellectual disabilities.

MORE WORK AHEAD

The successes in the 1970s and 1980s helped people with disabilities achieve access in different areas of life. During this time, the stigma of having a disability began fading. And thanks to those advancements, people with disabilities began enjoying greater access to resources. The fight for access was succeeding. However, while much had been accomplished, more needed to be done. The stage was set for comprehensive legislation to further facilitate that access. Challenges existed, and disability rights supporters rose up to take those challenges head-on.

CHAPTER FIVE

A GREAT IDEA

Disability rights activist, Rosie King, is a young adult whose illustrations appear in the children's books her mother Sharon King writes. She is also a writer who has penned magazine articles and several scripts for a television program. King plans to study creative writing in university, but also dreams of being an actress and storyteller. She lives in the United Kingdom, where she has become known as a skilled public speaker and a fierce advocate for people with disabilities, especially autism. At age nine, she was diagnosed with Asperger's syndrome, a type of autism that affects one's ability to effectively communicate and socialize. Ever since, King's been on a mission to help people better understand the condition. She challenges stereotypes that assume all people with autism have the same symptoms or experiences. She knows they do not because her younger siblings, who have autism, are nonverbal.

As a disability rights activist, King challenges the world's meaning of what is "normal," and

Mobility assistance dogs help with all kinds of tasks, including operating lights, opening and closing doors, retrieving items, pushing automatic buttons, and getting help in case of emergencies.

encourages others to accept differences. She presented a TEDMED 2014 talk titled "How autism freed me to be myself." The video of her presentation has been viewed more than two million times. In it, Rosie challenges viewers to redefine their version of normal by stating, "But if you think about it, what is normal? What does it mean? Imagine if that was the best compliment you ever received."

AT YOUR SERVICE

In January 2018, an airline passenger attracted much attention when attempting to bring a peacock on board with her. She said the creature was an emotional support animal needed for the journey. Emotional support animals are untrained, and used mainly for comfort. Service animals, on the other hand, receive special training to help or do work for a person with a disability. Because of their training, they are less affected by things that would distract, disturb, or distress other animals. People sometimes want to touch service animals, but that's not a good idea. They are working dogs, not pets, and need to focus in order to help their person.

Service animals are vital to a person's ability to function well indoors and out. Under the Americans with Disabilities Act, they have the right to accompany their person where other animals cannot go. By law, service animals can enter schools, businesses, and theaters, as well as travel on buses, trains, and flights. The access granted to service animals is a direct result of the successful fight for disability rights.

A WALL OF EXCLUSION

The fight for disabilities has always challenged the meaning of normal. It has focused on helping people expand their definitions and embrace differences. Key legislation has made it even easier. US President George H. W. Bush signed the Americans with Disabilities Act (ADA) into law on July 26, 1990. Three months later, on October 30, 1990, he signed the Individuals with Disabilities Education Act (IDEA) into law.

CELEBRATING THE ADA

The ADA is different from all other disability legislation in that it is a federal civil rights law. It assures that people with disabilities have protected rights, which every city and state must protect. According to the ADA's mission statement, its purpose is "to provide a clear and comprehensive mandate for the elimination of discrimination against individuals with disabilities." Hence, it provides a legal ground for preventing discrimination based on a disabling condition. And it is effective in stopping such discrimination when it occurs. The ADA threw open the door for people of all ages with disabilities to live freely and fully in society, enjoying the same rights, privileges, and access as other citizens. At its heart is independence and access. The ADA is designed to help people with disabilities live independently, not limited by a disability because of restricted access to service or opportunities. Thus, the ADA covers many of the areas that disability rights advocates have long sought after, including employment, housing, transportation, public services, telecommunications, and business services.

The ADA didn't happen overnight. It took a great deal of combined efforts, over many decades. Even then, the bill did not become law immediately. It was first introduced in Congress in 1988 and revised many times over the next two years. Many people across the country wanted to offer input, as the proposed legislation would have far-reaching effects. People with disabilities, disability rights advocates, organizations, business owners, and religious groups all expressed their views, curious about what it would require of them. Advocates wanted to make sure the law would address long-standing concerns, while organizations were concerned about the costs of reconstructive changes. Their collective input led to a final bill, which was passed by Congress.

The ADA's passage was cause for celebration. Three thousand people showed up in Washington, DC, to witness the signing. Seated at a table

The signing of the Americans with Disabilities Act inspired thousands of activists to gather on the White House's South Lawn. US president George H. W. Bush and his wife, Barbara, greet activists.

on the South Lawn of the White House, President Bush signed the ADA into law, as people watched with excitement. In his remarks, the president noted: "With today's signing of the landmark Americans with Disabilities Act, every man, woman, and child with a disability can now pass through once-closed doors into a bright new era of equality, independence, and freedom." Concluding his remarks, Bush added, "Let the shameful wall of exclusion finally come tumbling down."

AN EDUCATIONAL IDEA

Months after the ADA became law, President Bush also signed into law an expanded version of Public Law 94-142. It is called the Individuals with Disabilities Education Act (IDEA), Public Law 101-476. In their book, *The Complete Learning Disabilities Handbook*, Joan M. Harwell and Rebecca Williams Jackson explain that "IDEA redefined the definition of a learning disability." They continue: "The definition also states who is included and who will be excluded from special education services under the label 'learning disabled'."

Public Law 94-142 focused on providing a learning environment free from restrictions for students with varying disabilities. IDEA made it possible for infants and toddlers to also receive educational services. The law also allows for additional funds to help schools meet the needs of students with disabilities. IDEA significantly expanded the types of disabilities covered. Section 504 of the 1973 Rehabilitation Act focused on services for kids with mental or physical impairments. According to authors Harwell and Williams, IDEA expanded categories to include:

- Specific learning disability
- Speech impairment

- Seriously emotionally disturbed
- Traumatic brain injury
- Autism

Such specific listings make it easier for students to get educational services. Students and their families can more easily get assistance. They also recognize disabilities as a broad umbrella for many, many conditions that fall beneath it. Learning disabilities are finally getting more attention, and that is good for the student population with varying disabilities.

A WORKPLACE CHAMPION

Dr. Henry Viscardi, Jr. was a long-time champion of disability rights, especially for workers. His own work was inspired by the fact that he had been born without legs in 1912. A young Viscardi spent years in a hospital, as it was a time when society relegated people with disabilities to hospitals or other institutions. Things changed for Viscardi when he was fitted for prosthetic legs, but he never forgot his experience as a boy. In 1952, he started Abilities, Inc.

Its workers were mainly people with disabilities, an unusual workforce for the time. In 1962, he started the Human Resources School, later renamed for Viscardi in 1991. From the beginning, the school offered a complete educational experience, supporting students with disabilities. The school relies on advanced technology, adaptive sports, and other features to help students excel academically. Among other things, Viscardi also served as advisor to several presidents, and is credited with influencing laws that expanded disability rights. Viscardi died on April 14, 2004.

Dr. Henry Viscardi Jr. (*right*) advised presidents, including US president Jimmy Carter (*center*). Jack F. Smith, executive director of the White House Conference on Handicapped Individuals, joins them on the left.

DEVELOPMENTS AND STRIDES

Since the ADA became law, many new developments have led to increased independence and access for people with disabilities. Throughout the remainder of the 1990s other advancements were achieved in the fight for disability rights. In 1995, Paul Hearne created the American Association of People with Disabilities (AAPD). The AAPD brings together people with disabilities and their allies to work together to implement the goals of ADA. The next year, the Telecommunications Act became law. It required that equipment be accessible to people with disabilities. The Act made great strides in determining how mobile devices, computers, and other technology are designed.

ADDRESSING SUICIDE

Many people with disabilities struggle with self-esteem and self-confidence issues. Others struggle with feelings of worthlessness, because of how they are treated. In response, some have committed suicide. Some have even sought assisted suicide, the highly controversial act in which a medical professional provides a prescription drug to help a person die. Many people with disabilities, especially disability advocates, believe that assisted suicide is not the answer. They feel that the procedure further stigmatizes disabilities, making it seem as if a person has no reason to live because of his or her condition. For this reason, disability rights advocates began "Not Dead Yet" in 1996, a movement that opposes assisted suicides. The National Suicide Prevention hotline can be helpful, as it has counselors and capabilities to assist those who are hearing impaired or deaf. Contact (800) 273-8255 or suicidepreventionlifeline.org for assistance.

INSTITUTIONALIZED NO MORE

The 1990s came to an end with the development of a Supreme Court case *Olmstead v. L.C.* (1999). The Supreme Court is the highest court in the United States, and its laws must be followed by cities and states. The court ruled against unnecessarily institutionalizing people with disabilities, which had been what society did to hide people in mental hospitals and other facilities. The *Olmstead* case was a triumphant ending to a decade that saw continued advancement in disability rights. It reflected changing opinions and helped to usher in the new century.

CHAPTER SIX

STILL FIGHTING

Actor Christopher Reeve was best known for his roles in the *Superman* movies. His career changed after a horseback-riding accident in 1995 injured his spinal cord, leaving him paralyzed. The accident shocked the world. Reeve was loved by fans, and many of them fervently hoped that he would walk again. He did not. Reeve was a paraplegic for the remainder of his life.

In an interview on *The Oprah Winfrey Show*, Reeve admitted that he had played a paraplegic in a movie just months before his injury and was glad he was not paralyzed in real life. After the accident, he realized how suddenly a disability can occur. He told host Oprah Winfrey, "Any one of us could get hurt at any moment." Reeve and his wife, Dana, became greatly involved in the fight for disability rights. He used his fame as a platform to emphasize the importance of helping people with disabilities. With his wife, he started the Christopher & Dana Reeve Foundation to support others who have suffered spinal cord injuries.

After a horseback-riding accident left actor Christopher Reeve paralyzed, he and his wife, Dana, devoted the rest of their lives to helping fund research for spinal cord injuries.

They financially backed research that would lead to a cure. Although Reeve died in 2004 of cardiac arrest, and his wife died later that year from lung cancer, the Foundation continues its work.

The unexpected and severe nature of Reeve's injury helps people understand several facts about disabilities. First, it proved how some sports accidents lead to disabilities. Second, it revealed that disabilities happen to all people, even those who are famous and wealthy. And third, it underscored the need for more compassion for people with disabilities.

NAVIGATING WITH SUCCESS SIGNS

People with disabilities need compassionate relatives, friends, neighbors, and allies who care about their daily trials and triumphs. Increased compassion is an outcome of the fight for disability rights that cannot be measured. What can be measured is the success of activism. It is evident across industries where access is granted more than in the past. The result? People with disabilities can more easily navigate their communities and the country, thanks to these advances:

The fight for disability rights has spurred the increased use of braille lettering, making local and national sites more accessible for people with vision loss.

- Beeping crosswalk lights and neighbor-hood signage
- Curb cuts to make sidewalks accessible
- Special signage that indicates a facility is accessible to people with disabilities
- Handicapped parking spaces
- Front-of-the-bus seating for people with disabilities
- Accessible bathrooms in schools, hotels, theaters, workplaces, and other venues
- Ramps for walking or wheelchair use

While primarily benefiting people with disabilities, all of these improvements have helped community members across the country.

TWENTY-FIRST CENTURY ISSUES

With the success of the fight for disability rights, there are remaining issues underscoring the need for continued activism. Pressing issues in the twenty-first century include health care, abuse of people with disabilities, sports related injuries, and accessible technology.

HEALTH CARE

People with disabilities have varying needs for medicine, equipment, and therapies. One area of concern relates to the rights of patients and their families while receiving care, including the right to die. One of the most impactful cases involved Theresa Marie (known as Terri) and Michael Schiavo. Terri went into cardiac arrest in 1990, and sustained irreversible brain damage. A few months later, doctors said her condition would never improve. Nonetheless, they tried various medical strategies to treat her. Eventually, her husband sued to end her medical care in 1990, believing she would not have wanted to live the rest of her life on machines. He wanted her feeding tube to be removed, but her parents objected. The dispute lasted for fifteen years. Finally, he won the lawsuit, and his wife's feeding tube was removed on March 18, 2005. She died a few weeks later on March 31. The controversial case sparked great debate from people involved in various types of activism, including disability rights.

Another major health care concern has been access and affordability, and the fight for disability rights has made it easier for youths and adults to get care. A significant law that impacted disability rights was the Patient Protection and Affordability Care Act (ACA). It was signed into law by President Barack

Obama in 2010 and is also known as Obamacare, sometimes by those who opposed the law. Controversy has arisen over the ACA and its provisions, however, it has helped people with preexisting conditions. A preexisting condition is anything that a person has before having insurance, including disabilities. Also, the ACA expanded benefits to students, allowing them to stay on a parent or guardian's health care insurance up to age twenty-six.

People with disabilities who receive health benefits under state and federal health care insurance have been active in trying to protect their benefits. For example, the disabilities rights group, ADAPT, organized protests in 2011 to bring awareness to proposed changes in Medicaid, a state-run program that helps low-income adults, children, pregnant women, elderly adults, and people with disabilities in the United States. ADAPT relied on social media, among other strategies, to share their message. In the years to follow, other such groups staged similar demonstrations in Washington, DC, to protest future budget cuts.

STOPPING THE ABUSE

People with disabilities can be at greater risk for abuse, and advocates have called for additional protections. States responded, as was the case in 2012 when New York Governor Mario Cuomo and legislators created the Justice Center for Protection of People with Disabilities. In 2013, a successful lawsuit, *EEOC v. Hill Country Farms*, addressed the verbal and physical abuse of people with intellectual disabilities. It involved Hill

PREVENTING DISABILITIES

Sometimes, accidental injuries and illnesses can be prevented. Examples include the elderly, who are at high risk for falling, and those who do not wear protective gear while at play. Injury-related disabilities can be prevented by:

- Focusing on safety first. Handrails and seats in bathrooms can help prevent the elderly or people with disabilities from slipping or falling.
- Using health aids. Wearing prescribed hearing aids or eyeglasses helps to prevent injuries when a person can't hear or see.
- Using safety equipment. Helmets and padding for the knees and elbows may prevent injuries for those playing sports or riding skateboards and bikes.

(continued on the next page)

(continued from the previous page)

- **Taking care of one's health. Not smoking, eating properly, and exercising may prevent smoking- or obesity-related disabilities.**
- **Taking medicine, as prescribed. If the instructions of prescribed medication are not followed, it could result in irreversible physical, mental, or emotional harm. This can lead to short- or long-term disabilities.**

Disabilities can result from sports-related accidents, and activists are focusing on the need for continued research on such injuries. Safety equipment is always recommended when engaging in sports and recreational activities.

Country Farms, and its treatment of its employees with disabilities. The case was another key victory in the fight for disability rights.

SPORTS-RELATED INJURIES

Sports-related injuries have become a major concern, especially as football players sustain traumatic brain injuries. The National Football League (NFL) is addressing this matter, thanks in part to compassionate activists. Research is determining how brain injuries occur, and how they can be prevented in athletes of all ages. Some professional athletes have even donated their brains to science to advance research after their deaths.

ESTABLISHING ACCESSIBLE TECHNOLOGY

In an increasingly connected world, people with disabilities need technology that can easily connect them to the world. One important law is the Twenty-First Century Communications and Video Accessibility Act (CVAA). It was passed in 2010, making sure that access granted in earlier laws was applied to modern technology. The CVAA affects the use of computers and mobile devices and includes text and instant messaging, email, video technology, websites, and access to web browsers on mobile devices.

WHY STILL FIGHT?

Some of the advances for people with disabilities in the twenty-first century have been tremendous. People have enjoyed unprecedented access to resources, making life easier at home, school, and work. So why continue the fight? Because nothing is guaranteed. As new issues arise across different areas of life, people with disabilities could be impacted, and their rights could be affected. One example involves interactions with law enforcement. People with disabilities are prone to needing assistance from community helpers, like law enforcement, more than other citizens. However, many officers are not trained on how to communicate and interact with people with disabilities. A case in Maryland illustrates what can happen.

Ethan Saylor had Down syndrome. While in a movie theater, he was approached by off-duty officers asking him to leave after the movie. When he did not, he was arrested. While in police custody, Saylor was restrained, and died from an injury on January 12, 2013. The incident sparked controversy, in part because Saylor admired law enforcement officers. Had the officers understood Saylor's disability and had they been in uniform, it is possible that the incident would never have escalated, and Saylor would still be alive. As a result, Maryland established a commission to address the issue. It also passed a bill, establishing the Ethan Saylor Alliance for Self-Advocates as Educators in early 2015. The program's goal is to increase training for law enforcement about the needs of people with developmental and intellectual disabilities.

Every successful movement includes people of different genders, ages, races, and abilities working together. As in the past, teens are needed to help join the fight for disability rights. Getting involved helps people with disabilities and the community at large, regardless of whether or not a teen has a disability.

CHAPTER SEVEN

GET INVOLVED

M amie Cax's hair is close-shaven, her makeup is flawless, and she is fashionably dressed, down to the intricately designed cover on her prosthetic leg. Today, the blogger and disability rights advocate is the epitome of beauty and confidence. However, she did not always feel this way. At age fourteen, Mamie had cancer, and her leg was amputated. From then on, she hid the prosthetic leg she uses to walk. After college, though, her life changed when she connected online with others who had amputations. Cax soon found the strength and confidence to accept her difference. In an article on Yahoo.com honoring the United Nation's International Day of Persons with Disabilities, Cax noted, "I thought, wouldn't life just be easier if I accepted this and didn't have to hide it?" She acted on that thought, and stopped hiding her prosthetic leg. She later learned about, and started wearing, fashion accessories that cover, but do not hide, her leg.

Mamie Cax is known for the fashionable covers she wears on her prosthetic leg and for her body-positivity activism, which inspires others with physical disabilities.

Today, Cax is recognized as a person who helps other people with disabilities find the confidence they need to embrace their differences. Her body-positivity messages resonate with people with disabilities, as well as with those who do not have a disabling condition. Cax's experience reveals three things about living with a disability. First, a condition can result in an unexpected loss of a limb. Second, overcoming limitations related to disability often includes working on one's confidence and esteem. And third, self-acceptance is a key to thriving as a person with a disability.

GET INVOLVED

There are myriad opportunities for socially conscious teens, with and without disabilities, to get involved in the fight for disability rights. But before they do, it is important to note that there are some sacrifices that go along with involvement. One example is time. Teens will have to consider how much time they have to help people with disabilities. How can teens find the time? They can elect activism over working part-time jobs, hanging out with friends who aren't as passionate about the fight, or forgo sports or club activities to spend more time on disability-related issues. But the sacrifices of involvement are minor compared to the many benefits teens can enjoy as they engage in the fight for disability rights. Some benefits include:

- **Ample opportunities.** There are many causes with which a teen can become involved, including those of personal interest, or those they feel will allow them to have the greatest impact in their local area.
- **Expanded knowledge.** Some teens know very little about disabilities. Even teens with disabilities may not know much about other conditions. Teens can learn more about disabilities and how to help affected people when they join the fight for disability rights.
- **Service hours.** Many teens need service hours to graduate. Sometimes it's difficult to choose what to do. Many times, there are organizations that need help but are often overlooked. Teens can work with their schools to determine which organizations qualify for earning service hours.
- **Career exposure.** Activism often leads to awareness of future career choices. When teens learn about different aspects of the disability rights movement and issues involved, they glean knowledge and skills that can lead to more informed career choices.
- **Financial benefits.** Some organizations offer internships for participating in certain

programs, especially to college students.
- **Personal satisfaction.** Helping others sparks a sense of pride in one's service to people and communities.

EVERYONE IS WELCOME

Teens of all ages are needed, and teens of all abilities are welcome. Youths with disabilities can receive valuable information from working alongside activists whose work directly impacts them. When teens work alongside mentors with disabilities, they receive invaluable experience from others who understand their unique life experiences. At the same time, teens without disabilities are equally needed and can help in various ways. In some instances, they are needed to work with other students as mentors and helpers. When participating teens of all abilities bring enthusiasm, positive attitudes, and a willingness to learn to their activism, they directly influence the fight for disability rights.

KEYS TO SUCCESSFUL INVOLVEMENT

Choosing a location is one of the main keys to successful involvement. Opportunities exist locally, nationally, and internationally. Schools and organizations like Scouts BSA and Girl Scouts may be good resources for working with local or regional residents with disabilities. Local nursing homes and institutions that serve the elderly often welcome student groups. Hospitals, such as Shriners Hospitals for Children, serve people with disabilities and benefit from student volunteers who help behind the scenes and provide support to patients and their families.

Key Club International, a self-governing, student-led organization, offers ways for students to receive training from adult mentors and serve others in their schools and communities. Best Buddies has national and international clubs that team students without disabilities with their peers with intellectual and developmental disabilities. Online opportunities may also exist with other organizations. For example, teens may be able to get involved in online mentoring or tutoring opportunities. As would-be activists consider their participation, it's important to consider the following:

- **Safety first.** Activism can be exciting and rewarding, but wise participation means focusing on safety first. Teens should seek involvement that is not risky to their well-being, including their bodies, minds,

Participating in sports events, such as the Special Olympics World Games, lets athletes with intellectual disabilities, like Agnes Lekaleka of Malawi (in the lead), compete against their peers.

and emotions. If in doubt, don't do it.

- **Find a cause.** A good rule of thumb is to seek causes that are related to one's interests or passions. For example, students who love sports can seek out organizations like the Special Olympics as it focuses on making sports more accessible to people with disabilities. Another option is to link volunteerism with a passion, such as homelessness or food scarcity and hunger, which also affects people with disabilities. Shelters and food banks always welcome helping hands.

- **Find a perfect match.** Special interests can focus activism. For example, students who enjoy the arts can look for organizations that bring music, dance, photography, and the fine arts to people with disabilities.
- **Make it personal.** Teens can get involved with issues affecting them or someone they know. Teens looking to connect with organizations, can consider opportunities connected with local or national groups. Those could include the American Heart Association, the American Lung Association, Autism Speaks, and Alzheimer's Association.

SERVING FROM PERSONAL EXPERIENCE

The fear of spreading HIV/AIDS was rampant in the 1980s, partly due to misinformation about how the disease can be contracted. HIV (human immunodeficiency virus) affects the immune system, and AIDS (acquired immune deficiency syndrome) is the worst form of the virus. Over the years, activism has helped to shed light on

the transmission and treatments regarding HIV/
AIDS. Yet, a stigma still lingers. Activist Hydeia
Broadbent is dedicated to spreading awareness
and prevention strategies. She was born with HIV,
but she was not diagnosed until she was three
years old. Her story became well known, featured
extensively on news programs. As she grew, she
became a fierce advocate for sharing her story,
helping to fight the stigma, and promoting prevention by encouraging abstinence, and other
methods, to reduce the risk of transmission.

- **Team up.** Teaming up with like-minded,
  trusted adults and other teens help to
  make activism more meaningful for socially
  conscious teens. Plus, there is safety in
  numbers when doing advocacy. Teens do
  not need to worry about personal safety if
  they work with a team.
- **Start something.** Some schools have disability advocacy clubs. Teens can join those,
  and become more involved in the fight for
  disability rights. Or, they can talk with a guid-
  ance counselor or other administrator about
  starting a club in their school.
- **Be committed.** Commitment is a must for any
  activism to succeed. Teens should choose

how they want to be involved and remained committed. When they choose a schedule that works for them and stick to it, they make fighting for disability rights a priority.

A FIGHTING CHANCE

The fight for disability rights has changed, and continues to change, how people with disabili-

Teens can team up with their peers to join in the fight for disability rights, while addressing causes that are related to their interests.

SERVICE AFTER HIGH SCHOOL

Many universities offer opportunities to get involved in the fight for disability rights. Some offer clubs for students with disabilities, enabling them to connect with other students with a variety of conditions. In addition to camaraderie, they offer different services to help students succeed at college.

Other organizations also provide a change to engage in advocacy. The American Association of People with Disabilities (AAPD) offers a summer internship for college students interested in advocacy. Additionally, Active Minds is an organization that enables "students to speak openly about mental health in order to educate others and encourage help-seeking." Students can join local chapters near home or school and get involved in group activities.

ties are viewed and treated. It has lifted much of the stigma attached to having a disability. However, years of activism have proven that stigmas do not simply disappear. Rather, they must be challenged through accurate information and action. More activism is needed to help people with disabilities live as citizens not bound by stigmas associated with their conditions. And barriers need to be recognized, addressed, and removed!

Many advances have changed the playing field for people with disabilities. Exciting new breakthroughs keep the fight alive, including activities such as Disability Pride Parades. The first parade was in Chicago, Illinois, in 2004. It's since been held in multiples cities over the years. Additional developments came in 2013 when the US Department of Education started requiring schools to make "reasonable modifications." These modifications allowed students

It's easier than ever for people with disabilities to use computers and other technology, because of improvements resulting from the fight for disability rights.

with disabilities to play on traditional teams or provide parallel ones. This threw open a big door of opportunity for students who have long wanted to play, but could not. Enforcement of US disability rights also help. For example, in 2016, three European airlines were fined for not following US laws regarding access for people with disabilities. The fines are proof positive that the United States will not tolerate any entity—national or international—from blocking access for people with disabilities.

Indeed, since the Americans with Disabilities Act became law, many new developments have led to increased independence and access for people with disabilities. These include the following:

- More cars and trucks are equipped with special features so that people with physical disabilities can drive.
- Theaters have special sections for wheelchairs so moviegoers can be comfortable while viewing a film.
- Many cities offer low-cost, accessible van transportation services that take people wherever they want to go, including medical appointments and grocery shopping.
- Technology is more accessible than ever. Voice-to-text programs make it easier for people with disabilities to use mobile devices and computers.

- Industries have expanded access. For example, in 2012, thanks to efforts by the National Association of the Deaf, Netflix agreed to provide captions for all Netflix shows.
- Many colleges offer services to students with learning disabilities during the application process and additional services to those enrolled.

GET STARTED TODAY

People with disabilities have the right to live free from discrimination, prejudice, bullying, ridicule, and other cruel treatment. Historically, though, that is how people with disabilities were treated. Once called the ugliest woman in the world, Lizzie Velasquez is redefining beauty. She is also providing incentive for other people with—and without—disabilities to overcome perceptions and limitations. In her TEDx talk about the horrific cyberbullying she faced, Velasquez said: "In my mind, the best way that I could get back at all those people who made fun of me, who teased me, who called me ugly, who called me a monster, was to make myself better and ... use them as a ladder to climb up to my goals. That's what I did." When socially conscious teens join the fight for disability rights, they help people with disabilities to climb higher and reach their goals.

It's easy to get hyped about joining a cause. It's harder to fight the distractions that hinder participation. Lots of teens get excited and do nothing. A primary reason is that they forget to make activism an immediate goal. Teens can overcome this obstacle by choosing to start today. How? By making a plan to gather information, express an interest in participation, teaming up with peers and mentors, and immediately joining the fight for disability rights.

TIMELINE

1864 Gallaudet University opens in Washington, DC, as the first university for students with hearing loss, particularly those who are deaf.

1938 US President Franklin D. Roosevelt founds the National Foundation for Infantile Paralysis, now called the March of Dimes.

1940 Jacobus tenBroek and others establish the National Foundation for the Blind in Wilkes-Barre, Pennsylvania.

1950–1960s The civil rights movement's success inspires disability rights activists to fight for disability rights using many of the same effective strategies.

1964 US president Lyndon Johnson signs the Civil Rights Act, granting widespread protection against discrimination in the United States.

1970 Judy Heumann establishes Disabled in Action (DIA).

1972 Ed Roberts begins the Berkeley Center for Independent Living to address growing needs for resources for people with disabilities.

1973 Congress passes the Rehabilitation Act of 1973.

1988 Gallaudet University students' successful protests leads to the hiring of its first president with a disability.

1990 US president George H. W. Bush signs the Americans with Disabilities Act (ADA), a civil rights law.

President Bush also signs the Individuals with Disabilities Education Act (IDEA), redefining learning disabilities.

1995 The American Association of People with Disabilities is established.

1996 Passage of the Telecommunications Acts leads to more accessible equipment, including mobile devices and computers.

2010 Congress passes the Twenty-First Century Communications and Video Accessibility Act (CVAA) to expand access and address new types of communications practices and devices.

US president Barack Obama signs the Patient Protection and Affordability Care Act (commonly called "ACA") into law expanding health care coverage for US citizens.

2013 The US Department of Education requires schools to provide sports for students with disabilities.

GLOSSARY

abstinence The act of refraining from an activity, such as sex.

accessible Something that is easily used, reached, or entered.

advocate A supporter or helper, someone who helps bring about change.

allergen Anything to which a person is allergic.

amputate To remove a limb, usually by surgery.

attention deficit hyperactivity disorder (ADHD) A disability affecting attention and self-control.

autism A developmental disability affecting how a person communicates, or interacts with other people.

bipolar disorder A disability that affects a person's behavior and mood and which has been diagnosed by a doctor.

cardiac arrest An instance when the heart suddenly stops beating.

cerebral palsy A congenital disability that affects a person's muscles and movement.

congenital Something that a person is born with.

dyslexia A disability associated with difficulty reading.

epitome The essence of something.

gene A part of the smallest units in the body called cells; genes determine how something looks or grows and can be inherited from a family member.

grant Nonrepayable monies given by the

government or a corporation to an individual or organization to fund a specific project.

lunar Something that looks like or relates to the moon.

marginalize To render a person or group of people powerless or insignificant.

obsessive-compulsive disorder (OCD) An anxiety-related disability, usually seen in a person's repeated actions.

poliomyelitis/polio A virus caused by an infection, which temporarily or permanently paralyzes a person.

prosthetic An artificial device that replaces a body part, such as an arm or leg.

quadriplegic A disability causing all of a person's limbs to be paralyzed.

seizure The physical result of an abnormal brain activity, common in people with brain disorders such as epilepsy.

FOR MORE INFORMATION

Dialogue in the Dark
Corporate Communications
Dialogue Social Enterprise GmbH
Alter Wandrahm 5
20457 Hamburg
Germany
E-Mail: info@dialogue-se.com
Website: http://www.dialogue-in-the-dark.com
Facebook: @dialogueinthedar
Twitter: @DialogueSE
Dialogue in the Dark seeks to "change the mindset
of the general public on disability and diversity
and to increase tolerance for 'otherness' and
offer employment opportunities around the world.

Disabled Sports
451 Hungerford Drive, Suite 608
Rockville, MD 20850
(301) 217-0960
Email: info@dsusa.org
Website: https://www.disabledsportsusa.org
Facebook: @DisabledSportsUSA
Twitter: @DisabledSportUS
YouTube: DisabledSportsUS
Provides opportunities for participation in sports
for youth and adults with permanent disabili-
ties, including youth and wounded military.

Entry Point! at the American Association for the
    Advancement of Science (AAAS)
1200 New York Avenue NW
Washington, DC 20005
(202) 326-6600
Email: lsummers@aaas.org
Website: https://www.aaas.org
Facebook: @AAS.Science
Twitter: @AAAS
YouTube: wwwAAASorg
Entry Point!, an internship program offered by the
    AAAS, provides college students with STEM and
    business internships and co-op opportunities.

Mood Disorders Association of Ontario (MDAO)
36 Eglinton Avenue West, Suite 602
Toronto, ON M4R 1A1
Canada
(866) 363-MOOD (6663)
Website: http://www.mooddisorders.ca
Facebook: @MoodDisordersAssociationON
Instagram: mooddisordersassociation
Twitter: @mooddisorderson
MDAO offers free resources and programs for
    people with mood disorders, including fact
    sheets, webinars, videos, inspirational stories,
    and information about community support
    groups, such as "Youth Living Well" (for ages
    sixteen to twenty-nine).

Museum of disABILITY History
3826 Main Street
Buffalo, NY 14226
(716) 629-3626
Website: http://museumofdisability.org
Facebook:@museumofdisability
Twitter: @Musedisability
YouTube: MuseumofdisABILITY
Museum of disABILITY History provides on-site
    exhibits, collections, artifacts, and programs
    focused on increasing knowledge and under-
    standing of disabilities. Its website offers online
    resources, including a virtual museum, "Inside
    Scoop" pages on specific disabilities, and more.

National Association for the Deaf (NAD)
8630 Fenton Street, Suite 820
Silver Spring, MD 20910
(301) 587-1788
Email: nad.info@nad.org
Website: https://www.nad.org
Facebook and Twitter: @NAD1880
Instagram: @nad1880
YouTube: @NADvlogs
NAD is dedicated to helping people with hear-
    ing disabilities. Extensive resources, including
    information about its "Youth Leadership Pro-
    grams," help to inspire, inform, and prepare
    students to be leaders and advocates for those
    with hearing disabilities.

National Center for Learning Disabilities (NCLD)
32 Laight Street, Second Floor
New York, NY 10013
(212) 545-7510
Email: info@beyondbullies.org
Website: http://ncld.org
Facebook:@NCLD.org
Twitter: @ncldorg
YouTube: @NCLD1401
NCLD offers resources to people with disabilities,
    their parents, and professionals. Resources
    include information about its scholarships for
    high school students to attend college.

National Educational Association of Disabled
    Students (NEADS)
Rm. 514, Unicentre
1125 Colonel By Drive
Carleton University
Ottawa, ON K1S 5B6
Canada
(877) 670-1256
Email: info@neads.ca
Website: https://www.neads.ca
Facebook: @myNEADS
YouTube: @NEADS
NEADS provides school- and job-related tools for
    high school and college students, including
    information about transitioning from high

school, financial aid, employment, and accessibility on campus.

National Federation of the Blind
200 East Wells Street at Jernigan Place
Baltimore, MD 21230
(410) 659-9314
Website: https://nfb.org
Facebook: @NationalFederationoftheBlind
Twitter: @NFB_voice
YouTube: @NationsBlind
National Federation of the Blind provides extensive resources for people with vision-related disabilities. Services include advocacy letters and events.

Partners for Youth with Disabilities (PYD)
5 Middlesex Avenue, Suite 307
Somerville, MA 02145
(617) 556-4075
Email: info@pyd.org
Website: http://www.pyd.org
Facebook: @pydboston
Twitter: @PYDboston
PYD provides mentoring opportunities, job readiness, theater arts, and other inclusion resources for youth with disabilities.

FOR FURTHER READING

Blume, Judy. *Deenie*. New York, NY: Atheneum Books for Young Readers, 2014.

Burcaw, Shane. *Laughing at My Nightmare.* New York, NY: Square Fish, 2014.

Draper, Sharon M. *Out of My Mind.* New York, NY: Atheneum Books for Young Readers, 2012.

Haugen, David M., and Susan Musser, eds. *Disabilities.* (Teen Rights and Freedom). Farmington Hills, MI: Greenhaven Press, 2014.

King, Wesley. *OCDaniel.* New York, NY: Simon & Schuster/Paula Wiseman Books, 2017.

Landau, Jennifer. *Teen Voices: Real Teens Discuss Real Problems: Teens Talk About Learning Disabilities and Differences*. New York, NY: Rosen Publishing, 2018.

Leavitt, Amie Jane. *Service Learning for Teens: Helping People With Disabilities and Special Needs Through Service Learning.* New York, NY: Rosen Publishing, 2015.

Mayrock, Aija. *The Survival Guide to Bullying: Written by a Teen.* New York, NY: Scholastic, Inc., 2015.

Nichols, Susan. *Confronting Ableism. Speak Up! Confronting Discrimination in Your Daily Life.* New York, NY: Rosen Young Adult, 2018.

Palacio, R. J. *Wonder.* Movie Tie-In Edition. New York, NY: Alfred A. Knopf, 2017.

Velasquez, Lizzie. *Dare to Be Kind: How Extraordinary Compassion Can Transform Our World.* New York, NY: Hachette Book Group Inc., 2018.

BIBLIOGRAPHY

Burcaw, Shane. *Not So Different: What You REALLY Want to Ask About Having a Disability.* New York, NY: Roaring Book Press, 2017.

Center for Disability Information and Referral. "Kids Corner." Retrieved January 15, 2018. https://www.iidc.indiana.edu/cedir/kidsweb.

Disabled-world.com. "Disability Statistics: Information, Charts, Graphs and Tables." Retrieved March 4, 2018. https://www.disabled-world.com/disability/statistics.

Emmanuelsdream.weebly.com. "Emmanuel's Dream.org." Retrieved January 15, 2018. https://emmanuelsdream.weebly.com.

Equal Employment Opportunity Commission. "Remarks of President George Bush at the Signing of the Americans with Disabilities Act." Retrieved December 30, 2017. https://www.eeoc.gov/eeoc/history/35th/videos/ada_signing_text.html.

Ghosh, Shreersha. "Former Rugby Player Left Paralyzed for Life After Swallowing Slug As Dare." International Business Times, March 8, 2018. http://www.ibtimes.com/former-rugby-player-left-paralyzed-life-after-swallowing-slug-dare-2660801.

Harwell, Joan M., and Rebecca Williams Jackson. *The Complete Learning Disabilities Handbook. Ready-to-Use Strategies & Activities for Teaching Students with Learning Disabilities.* 3rd ed. San Francisco, CA: Jossey-Bass, 2008.

Jensen, Bart. "Airlines fined up to $550K for dis-
abilities complaints." *USA Today*, April 14,
2016. https://www.usatoday.com.

Johnson, Eric. "Disability Rights Activist Darius
Weems Loses Battle with Duchenne Muscular
Dystrophy." ABC News, October 10, 2016. http:
//abcnews.go.com/Health/disability-rights
-activist-darius-weems-loses-battle-duchenne
/story?id=42708683.

King, Rosie. "How autism freed me to be myself."
TedMed 2014, September 2, 2014. https://www
.ted.com/talks/rosie_king_how_autism_freed
_me_to_be_myself/transcript.

May Institute. "Developmental Disabilities Q&A."
MayInstitute.org, 2010. https://www
.mayinstitute.org/pdfs/developmental
_disabilities_fact_sheet.pdf.

Miller, Samantha. "The Real-Life Mom Moment That
Led to Emotional Bestseller (and Now Movie)
Wonder." *People*, November, 17, 2017.
http://people.com/movies/wonder-rj-palacio
-story-behind-book.

Peters, Terri. "Meet the first Gerber baby with
Down syndrome; his name is Lucas!" *Today
Show*, February 7, 2018. https://www.today
.com/parents/2018-gerber-baby-first-gerbe
r-baby-down-syndrome-t122258.

Scott, Brittany. "The 1977 Disability Rights Protest
That Broke Records and Change Laws."

Atlas Obscura, November 9, 2017. https://www
.atlasobscura.com/articles/504-sit-in-san
-francisco-1977-disability-rights-advocacy.

UN News. "Singer-songwriter Stevie Wonder des-
ignated UN Messenger of Peace." December 1,
2009. https://news.un.org/en/story
/2009/12/323032-singer-songwriter-stevie
-wonder-designated-un-messenger-peace.

US Centers for Disease Control and Prevention. "Disability Impacts ALL of Us." December 30, 2017.
https://www.cdc.gov/ncbddd/disabilityandhealth
/infographic-disability-impacts-all.html.

US Department of Labor. "Section 504, Rehabilitation Act of 1973." Retrieved March 4, 2017.
https://www.dol.gov/oasam/regs/statutes
/sec504.htm.

Velasquez, Lizze. "How Do YOU Define Yourself
Lizzie Velasquez at TEDxAustinWomen." You-
Tube.com, 13:10. Posted December 20, 2013.
https://youtu.be/c62Aqdlzvqk.

Viscardi Center, The. "A Brief History of Dr. Henry
Viscardi, Jr." YouTube.com, 2:37. Posted May 10,
2013. https://www.youtube.com
/watch?v=chHWh9QnqtU.

Wilkens, John. "A new ride for Emmanuel Yeboah."
San Diego Tribune, October 24, 2015. http://
www.sandiegouniontribune.com/lifestyle
/people/sdut-emmanuel-yeboah-ghana
-2015oct24-story.html.

INDEX

ABOUT THE AUTHOR

Lisa A. Crayton was born with a congenital absence of three left fingers, a fancy way of saying she was born with just two fingers on her left hand. She loves debunking myths about limitations, helping people understand disabilities, and encouraging people with disabilities to enjoy full lives. A former corporate publications editor and writer, she loves writing for children and teens. She also loves mentoring writers and especially enjoys speaking at writers' conferences. She earned a master of fine arts degree from National University and a bachelor's degree in public relations and journalism, cum laude, from Utica College.

PHOTO CREDITS